Updrafts

Steve Griffiths

Fair Acre Press

First published in Great Britain in August, 2020 by Fair Acre Press

www.fairacrepress.co.uk

A CIP catalogue record for this book is available from the British Library

ISBN 978-1-911048-46-6

Typeset & Cover design by Nadia Kingsley

Cover image © Paul Kielty 2020

About Steve Griffiths

Steve Griffiths was born and raised in Anglesey, spent his working life in London, and now lives in Ludlow. He published seven collections of poems between 1980 and 2016, all but the first with Seren Books and Cinnamon Press. Last year, his poetry was brought together in *Weathereye: Selected Poems* (2019). He has broadcast widely, and has read in several countries, including a series of seven readings in New York in 2012. He is one of the hundred twentieth-century Welsh poets writing in English featured in The Library of Wales' *Poetry 1900-2000* (2007, Parthian Books). His poems have appeared in many anthologies, most recently the NHS anthology *These are the Hands*. You can see filmed performances of his *Late Love Poems* on YouTube.

Steve was once a welfare rights worker in Islington, and later became a researcher and policymaker, writing area profiles of deprivation and health inequality across England, including Manchester, Walsall and six London boroughs. He has written four public health reports and a baseline study for reducing emergency hospital admissions. At the start of the century, he was one of the architects of a billion-pound annual investment in supported housing, much of it now taken apart. His poetry website is www.stevegriffithspoet.com

Previous Publications

Weathereye: Selected Poems (SilverWood Books 2019)
Late Love Poems (Cinnamon Press 2016)
Surfacing (Cinnamon Press 2011)
An Elusive State (Cinnamon Press 2008)

Acknowledgements

'First weeks' and 'The Gift' have appeared in *Stand*.
'The first Chinese spacewalker wanders off-message' in *Scintilla*.
'Saltings' was published on the Halen Môn – Anglesey Sea-Salt - website.
'Nigel Jenkins, poet, his death' appeared in 'Encounters with Nigel - Celebrating the life of Nigel Jenkins', Ed. Jon Gower, publ. H'mm Foundation, 2014.

Other poems appeared in 'Surfacing' (Cinnamon Press, 2011), 'Late Love Poems' (Cinnamon Press, 2016), and 'Weathereye: Selected Poems' (SilverWood Books, 2019).

Thanks are due to Ludlow Fringe 2020 for inspiration and encouragement.

Contents

Who brought me into the light

Those hills in their slow motion
undulation, their ripple of
shaken planes, their t'ai chi
celebratory whip of energy:
they are shaken sheets.

Who'll hold the corners
as they meet and fold?

Not my mother who taught me
to grip on in stiff wind
so they wouldn't tear
from my fingers and trail
in the grass.

Not my mother
who's long gone
but who showed me
the danced pattern of meeting
and folding, those waves
of light and shadow
on land, so quick on the sea,
a lifetime where I stand.

The first Chinese spacewalker wanders off-message

I'm suspended in no-air,
neither warm,
as down there
the white stone
above the rivulet
absorbs the heat
of the late afternoon;
nor chilled,
in the intimate
potency of shadows;
but regulated.

I see so clearly
how the moon's a coin;
the wide horizon's slot
an open goal.
Every time it does it,
drops in satisfyingly
and we're none the poorer for it.
Though time will come
to finish us, strewn
among spurned generosities,
there's something still

about the days' faultless turning
that refuses to diminish us.

Saltings

The taste that sea-salt
opens up:
its slow, white
               bolt
from the blue.

The taste you thought
just out of reach,
the memory you find
you never knew you'd lost.

Sardines newly caught on the beach.

Add seasalt to risotto.
It pulls you in towards
a chorus of ingredients,
the memory of sea
beneath them
as they make their entrance
and they sing,
the sea-bass
thrumming in the undertow
taut as a bass-string.

Sea-salt summoned
where the hawthorns lean
right over
under the determined
salt wind:
when you were little
it would hold you up
if you leaned
back on it.
The pleasure of the gust
sustained: blow, wind,
hold my body
upright, trusting,
behind me the west,
my lips awakened
to its taste.

Once you ran
to keep up
with a moving column
of sunbeams, listening
for the washing's crack
on the line,
the whip of sails.

Sheets hung out
on billows of Atlantic
wind. At night
they will enfold
your child's dreams
of salt, of scales
glistening.

It's brought in
from far out
where the sea churns,
runs, dances
into space, pulled
by the moon that brooks
no refusal.   Crystals
of seasalt glisten
up from a dish,
light without eyes
snagged on a sightline.
Just the salt and the moon:
unconsummated recognition.
They're miraculous,
those eyes that lock
across a meal
amid the blind
whisperings of light.

The project

To lay another deck
over unknowing, and another
is a lifetime's work,
to read, to think, to love
in layers, then to navigate
the moods of the wood:
there's a word
or a nail missing,
or a word too many
and there's all those
that are substitutes
for the real thing,
the grafts and counterfeits
to be assimilated.
The project's to pass through
the wounds of storms
with new corridors
and a sense of the inevitable,
simple, potent, complicated
as an old house or a tree,
and to read, to love, to think
for the first time again,
to penetrate the bark from within,
imagine that, drilling out
in the spring:
the dazzling new light
when you've been let go.

Lifetime

Night gathers
on the beach:
flecks of foam
race and fade
across the sand.

I wake surprised
to find the stars,
remote above the wind,
reach in.

Nigel Jenkins, poet, his death

An hour before I heard of his death
I saw a kingfisher in black and white
in a fold of January half-light.
It crossed the river away from me.
Wet noise closed in and I lost it:
something rare, keen-eyed
for stillness and every stirring,
welcome in surprised lives,
holding its flash of blue
bowstrung like a good word
for the right unleashing.

The gift

It was the kind of space
you'd be proud to work in.
The women looking out for each other
from the half dozen beds in the patient bay.
The one who'd fallen in the bathroom
at home after surgery
and broken tibia and knee
was the life and soul
as the sightlines were passed back and forth.
Those who left would remember her.
Staff, noticing,
out of the matrix of what made them.
You'd want to find something to bring to this.

To recreate it,
follow the trails
                        back up or down
from where healing poured like sunlight
to where each found
the gift to strengthen the gift.

What comes around

Just as you convince yourself
that what the weather does
is teach disappointment
there's a molten crack of light
that slices the midwinter horizon
below the last bulk of advancing rain.
It's what you believe.

Exercising

Exercising
flat on my back
on the floor,
one foot in the air,

head to the bay window,
in the clear blue sky above me
pass three herons, slow
and upside down over Harringay.

First weeks

I open to my mother's milk.

Milk is as light does.

The positives of the world
are composed
from this thin line
of unpredictability:

no joy but in recognition
and discovery.

No resilience
but in the delicate.

From *The Shelveian Event*

And to the south of Corndon Hill
whose Ordovician dolerite
piped the hot verticals
that to this day mushroom its cowl,
the Hyssington Volcanic Member,
acid vitroclastic tuffs,
sandstones, wackes;
and dreaming in the south
of distant time, breaking rhythm –
the Clun Forest Disturbance,
the heavy footstep of its thunderous glance.

A January wind
carves across Hyssington Marsh.
The clouds are whipped away,
the sky is clear.
I stare for hours at the thought
of raindrops' impact, baked
for posterity in seconds,
fossilised with care on mudflats
one by one in the tenderness
of moments hardly yet materialised.
The storm passed on,
the earth is harsh,
and came to something here.

Skylight

The skylight's just that:

lens to the fixed stars
over the ruminative clouds
the moon drives
in their indifferent grandeur
as if to milking;

little frame for the worlds
above my naked stillness
anchored on the rough cord
of a dark landing.

Rockpool

The pool is barren
where my net tracked shoals
of shrimps that drifted,
darted, distracted.
Fifty years ago
it was a screen
I penetrated
and that answered back,
though framed with moss
and braids of bladderwrack
like an antique certificate,
while yards away, the tight-lipped
waves relaxed and died:
replenish, diminish,
was the sound they made,
a pulsing background static
ready to augment
as soon as I was ready
to a human voice
that would begin to spread
among the rocks,
when I was six.

Ocean from space

Tides,
to and fro,
so
pendulum.
Hung water.

Earth's mauled,
fingered,
spun,
a draft scored over
till it's worn right through

and needs
to be composed
again,
once more
without a human face:

dusk's trawlnet
chases afternoons
across it
for the necklaces
of lives and waves

as they unravel,
iridescent.
Equilibrium
unlikely:
not in the lexicon.

Held in lightness
and in force,
earth stirs
in a draught
from some other spinning,

slippery,
slithering away
from this moment with us on.
Fine sentiments
are lit up

late

like cirrus from below the horizon.

Dark energy

I was drained,
my juices leeched away,
the battery neglected.
I think of the Humber Hawk
abandoned on a verge
up on the Mynd,
of its return to nature
under the settlements
of dark moss on the rust,
and the buzzard
with its still wings
waiting for the furtive rabbits'
loss of concentration.
Even in the image
of abandonment, optimism.
Shadows in the fields,
earth clutching shallow roots
sympathetically,
unregarded bolts of darkness
hold things together.

Flock roosting

All my sense
of the fluidity of form
comes from the November
shapeshifting
of fifteen hundred starlings
for the mathematical,
valedictory joy of it:
they turn in on themselves
in a glove
that fills the whole
dusk above the water,
and out, and in again
but where is the hand they enclose
before they contract
suddenly to roost
on a passive black geometry
of spars,
reflecting on the day
in their small individual
darknesses
beneath a pier,
joined by diminishing afterthoughts
from afar
to perfect their form
which is hidden,
trembles, chatters and is still?

The same place

The storm binges on after hours
through darkened isobars.
A tornado in Kensal Rise,
which rises as it must.
The wind is chest-thumpingly high
round the house on the hilltop
where you live, bathed in leaves
in their changing ways.
My love for the gale's deep-rooted
but this bracing howl's a test.
The timbers strain, the house slips
anchor, spins, slowly at first,
then I hear you chuckle under the quilt,
and I'm certain we belong within the same
point on the map, in the same
rumpled bed, on the same swirl of contours.

Rare honey

For Siôn Evans, beekeeper

Black fur, bulk
of the dwindling bee.
Chambers of sweet rock
glisten, trickle, giving
and crystalline, long
after the ruffle of wind
on the flight home.
Power melting on the tongue.

Spring

Viewed from above in early spring
the oaks have a shifting, softened quality
that gathers itself for green.
Spaced at our feet
the birdcalls rise at intervals
and the urgent, airy thump
of wingbeats punctuates
complaint with escape.

A rustle of wind
moves up the hill towards us,
recedes through the mix
of trees behind us, all
the senses awakened.

I had thought my capacity
for happiness was limited.
It is good to have arrived here
even if a little late,
discovering a language
I was exiled from,
waking with the ground
strewn with clouds and flowers
and images with their names
that are breaking cover, unafraid.

www.ingramcontent.com/pod-product-compliance
Lightning Source LLC
Chambersburg PA
CBHW051003030426

42339CB00007B/459